Wandering Woman:
Northern California

The Ultimate Road Trip: One Woman's Journey Across the United States by Car

Julie Bettendorf

Contents

Introduction

"Not all who wander are lost." JRR Tolkien

Are you sure? I thought to myself, as I tried not to panic. I was a long way from anything familiar, but that was how it should be. I had driven thousands of miles on dusty, pothole-filled roads. It's often on the worst roads that you can discover something truly amazing.

My dusty CRV was parked beside me, containing one restless dog and a variety of snack bags, all empty by now. There were no buildings in sight, no cars or people or movement at all. Only the constant humming of the insects as they buzzed around my head.

I turned to my left – another straight road that trailed off into the distance. I glanced over to the right, then behind me – two more barely discernible roads stretched out into the abyss. I was in a four-way intersection with no signs, no sense of direction, and no sign of life for several miles. No cell service either. *Damn*, I thought. *I'm lost.*

How did I get here? I couldn't help but feel like this little intersection was a cruel metaphor for life. I began to daydream, imagining each road might transport me back to a different time, a different role in my life, and a different me.

If I took the road from whence I came, it could lead me all the way back to Oregon, back to my cheating third husband, back to a life of loneliness and solitude. There is no greater loneliness than being married to someone who isn't actually present in your life.

If I took the road to my left, perhaps it could take me back to my career as a dental hygienist, a job I hated deep down in my soul. There is something so disengaging about cleaning teeth for a living. It's a disgusting, smelly way to get a paycheck. It pays well, which is great, but the best part is the huge gob of friends I enjoy to this day.

Or maybe the road to my right, *yes – maybe that's the path*, I imagined. Maybe it could take me back to my real treasure, my kids. Back to their smiling, innocent faces as toddlers, as they danced around the Christmas tree and their father and I were still married. Back when they still needed me for every little thing.

But, that was just it. I didn't feel needed anymore. My kids weren't toddlers anymore – they were both full-grown adults, and far too busy for me. My dental buddies were still working, but I wasn't. Dental hygiene had robbed me of the cartilage in my fingers, giving me severe, disabling arthritis. And, I wouldn't be returning to any more husbands either, because three marriages were quite enough for me.

All three of these paths, all three of these roles – the wife, the mother, and the dental hygienist – had seemingly been stripped from me within a year. I was lost and looking to find myself again.

The funny thing about this phrase, "not all who wander are lost" – is that, in my experience, wandering and being lost walk hand-in-hand with one another, and the expression can be flipped. In my experience, not all who are lost are wandering, and that is a real disservice to the beauty and clarity that the world has to offer.

When one becomes lost, wandering is the only option to guide oneself back to a path. After all, one could not come upon any dirt path at all without wandering.

I began wandering at an early age, both with my mind and with my feet. At eight years old, I was reading a book about archaeology and dreaming of one day seeing Egypt. I didn't follow a traditional path in high school either, going heavily into foreign languages, in hopes of one day using them.

At twenty-five years old, I divorced my first husband (the dental student who talked me into becoming a dental hygienist so I could work for him) and decided to give traveling a real shot. I took off for the Andes and Macchu Picchu, climbing up ancient Inca stone steps to reach the magnificent ruins.

Anyone who has been to Macchu Picchu will tell you there is something ethereal and deeply spiritual about the place. The ruins stretch out across the emerald green mountains, way up in the middle of the sky. Macchu Picchu gave me my first experience of feeling history. This trip inspired me to come back and complete a degree in archaeology, and I've been wandering ever since.

More travel followed including a backpack trip around Europe for three months, by myself, and trips to Britain, Italy, and Greece. I visited the burial places of Crusaders, mummies, and ancient kings. I happened upon the castle of my namesake in Bettendorf, Luxembourg, and wandered my way through European history.

My favorite excursion by far was finally seeing Egypt with my daughter in 2012. Just like my childhood dream envisioned, I rode a camel beneath the pyramids of Giza, with my head wrapped in some man's sweaty turban. It was perfect.

Traveling has always been my own personal antidote to pain. I went to Mexico after my first and second divorces, Canada after my third, and Italy after my dad died. Call it avoidance if you want, but I call it an accelerated form of healing in the purest sense of the word. I believe travel can heal your soul.

Wandering has always worked its wonders on me – made me feel renewed, rejoiceful, grateful, and purposeful. It's been my medicine.

So, as I stood in that intersection, I once again wondered how wandering had led me so astray this time. *What the hell am I supposed to do now?* It was then that I realized that one last path had not been considered yet – the path which stretched straight out in front of me. *Which role does this represent?* I pondered.

The answer smacked me in the face.

That last dirt road – the only path that could take me where I wanted to go, the only path that ever truly healed me or showed me the way – was the path of the traveler. The wife, the mother, and the hygienist roles – though valued in their time – were sitting in the bleachers now. It was time to welcome and enable my boldest, bravest, and perhaps most pivotal role yet:

The role of the Wandering Woman.

Welcome to Wandering Woman

This book is for you – the grieving empty nester mom, the be-grudged housewife, the woman in need of a drastic change in her life. Really, this book is for anyone with a passion for traveling. If you feel lost with no sense of direction or purpose in life, that's a bonus – this book will be even more appealing to you. And lastly, if you're a man reading this book, congratulations for holding a book with the word woman in the title. You're con-tributing to gender equality, and that's pretty neat.

I decided to combine three of my dearest loves – travel, history, and archaeology – and put them into a book because I believe wandering has the power to change your life. I have been to many areas of the world and had too many outstanding experiences to list. However, by the time both my children had

Me

moved out in 2017, I had never seen my own country – America. It was the perfect time to explore a new country (my own) and discover a new me at the same time.

So, I packed up my Honda CRV, along with some gear and my 14-year-old furry friend, Sadie. ***Wandering Woman*** is the chronicle of my journey across eleven states, discovering the joy of getting lost and finding myself along the way.

Why America?

A *merica, the beautiful?* I sure think so, but I didn't realize just how beautiful our country is until I embarked on traveling across eleven western states in a year.

The United States offers everything for the discerning palate. From spectacular beaches, austere mountains, to rolling plains, our country has it all. It's difficult to comprehend just how large and impressive our scenery is, until you experience it first-hand, with the ultimate road trip.

I also realized just how much of our history is missing from U.S. history I was taught as a kid. The history of our country didn't begin with the pilgrims landing on Plymouth Rock in the 1600s. Our history is far more ancient, with rock art and archaeological sites dating back over 12,000 years.

We also owe a tremendous debt to early pioneers who tamed our land. The Mormons and other groups ventured into the great unknown with their families and their worldly possessions. Some of them pulled cumbersome handcarts across the country to settle in inhospitable, dangerous locations.

The goal of Wandering Woman is to bring history back to life and make it interesting again. I am presenting some famous sites, and many little-known ones. You will take the road-less-traveled with me, while we explore ghost towns, rock art sites, archaeological sites, and museums, to discover the colorful tapestry that is our country.

I present some history, including dates, but my goal is to present more of the real-life stories of history, including ghost stories, profiles in history, voices from the past, and moments in time, to give you, the reader, a deeper understanding of the context of history.

This is by no means an exhaustive list of places to visit. In fact, I encourage you to discover America for yourself, as I did, by making a trek across the land by car. You can explore as the early explorers did, just a little more comfortably, with a lot less hardship.

I hope you enjoy this book and take a little time out to discover our beautiful country, and maybe even discover yourself in the process.

Safe Travels,

Julie Bettendorf

Welcome to Northern California

The Golden State

Northern California, so full of history. There is so much for everyone, and everyone knows it. From the historic gold rush towns, to spectacular wine country, Northern California has it all. It is truly the golden state.

5 things to love about Northern California:

- Scenic drives deep into California wine country

- Ghost towns like Bodie and Coloma

- Gold rush history sites like Marshall Gold Discovery

- Wonderful walkable areas like Old Town Sacramento

- Historic Spanish missions like Carmel Mission

Dreams of Northern California

"When California was wild, it was the floweriest part of the continent." **John Muir**

"California is a place of invention, a place of courage, a place of vision, a place of the future. People who made California what it is were willing to take risks, think outside convention and build." **Nicolas Berggruen**

"San Francisco is the only city I can think of that can survive all the things you people are doing to it and still look beautiful." — **Frank Lloyd Wright**

Favorite Stuff to See in Northern California

Favorite Ghost Towns:

- Bodie

- Coloma

Favorite Historical Sites:

- Marshall Gold Discovery State Historic Park

- Sonoma State Historic Park

Favorite Spanish Missions:

- Mission San Juan Bautista

- Carmel Mission

Favorite Scenic Drive:

- Hwy. 101 and Hwy. 1 coastal drives, Oregon and Northern California

Favorite Way to Spend an Afternoon:

- Walking through Monterey Bay Aquarium and Fisherman's Wharf in Monterey

Early Northern California

Early Carmel Mission

Early Monterey

Measuring Snowfall at Donner Pass

Lava Beds

T he ***Lava Beds National Monument*** is an amazing place, both for its history and its geology. There are over 850 documented caves here, more than any other area in the contiguous United States. The lava caves were created by an eruption at Mammoth Crater 32,000 years ago, sending molten lava 10 miles downhill. With the help of my friend, who is a Park Ranger and cave expert, I toured several caves including the **Catacombs Cave**, which is an astounding 6,903 feet long. My favorite was the **Skull Cave**, because it contains the skull of a bighorn sheep, placed there about 3000 years ago.

The lava beds have been inhabited for over 10,000 years by groups including the Modoc people. It was the Modocs who came into conflict with the army and white settlers. The conflict led to the Modocs signing a treaty to move to the Klamath Reservation in 1864. Life was hard on the reservation, with lack of supplies and infighting between the Modocs and the Klamaths, so the leader of the Modocs, "Captain Jack" led his people off of the reservation. A fight ensued, killing one soldier, and the Modocs fled to the Lava Beds.

The area known as ***Captain Jack's Stronghold*** is a fascinating section of the park. It was here that the leader of the Modocs, Kientpoos, nicknamed Captain Jack by the whites, held out against the army. Less than 60 Modoc warriors held out against an army of over 1000 men. Small groups of Modocs, including women, children, and elderly, were finally captured, after being half-starved.

The park also contains a small monument, known as ***Canby's Cross*** where General E.R.S. Canby was killed on the spot by Captain Jack. Canby was attempting to negotiate peace with the Modocs when he was killed. History indicates that Captain Jack did not want to kill Canby, but he was goaded into it by members of his tribe. <small>Lava Beds Natural History Association</small>

How to get to Lava Beds National Monument:

Lava Beds National Monument is located near the city of Tulelake at 1 Indian Well Heights

Profiles in history:

Kientpoos, or Captain Jack, was born in 1837. in a village along the Lost River in Oregon. He rose to prominence as a leader of the Modocs, and was one of the signers of the 1864 treaty of the Modocs, Klamath, and other tribes with the United States government. The purpose of the treaty was to move the native tribes on to the Klamath reservation. He soon found the reservation to be an inhospitable place, and the government failed to address the conditions. Captain Jack and his followers and warriors left the reservation and fled to the area of the Lava Beds National Monument. There, they held off a much larger army of U.S. soldiers. In an attempt at negotiating a peace treaty, Kientpoos killed two of the negotiators, Reverend Eleazar Thomas and Major General Edward R.S. Canby. Kientpoos was hanged, along with three other Modoc leaders at Fort Klamath on October 3, 1873. Kientpoos was the only Native American leader to be convicted as a war criminal.

Major General Edward R.S. Canby was born in 1817 in Kentucky. He participated in the Civil War and was stationed at Fort Defiance in New Mexico. Canby and his army defeated the confederates at the Battle of Glorietta Pass, forcing the confederates to flee to Texas. After the pivotal battle, Canby was promoted to brigadier general in 1862. He was reassigned to commander of the Pacific Northwest in 1873. Canby was murdered by the Modoc leader, Kientpoos, while attempting to negotiate a peace treaty. Major General Edward R.S. Canby was the highest-ranking general officer to die during the Indian Wars.

Ferndale

T he picturesque town of *Ferndale*, part of the lost coast of
California, is the town that time forgot. It was established in
1852 by two brothers, Seth and Stephen Shaw, who travelled by

canoe to the site which would be named Ferndale. The beautiful town contains a vast assortment of spectacular Victorian homes and buildings. The entire town of Ferndale is listed on the National Register of Historic Places. In 1880, Ferndale was a town known for its dairies. The dairy farmers grew wealthy and displayed their wealth by building ornate homes, known as Butterfat Palaces.

My favorite of these Butterfat Palaces is the wonderful Gingerbread Mansion, a spectacular combination of adornments. Now, the building is a bed and breakfast. Ferndale has served as a spot to film a few Hollywood movies, including Salem's Lot, Outbreak, and The Majestic. Renowned chef Guy Fieri was born in Ferndale. He got his start selling pretzels and washing dishes, to pay for a foreign exchange program to France, and the rest is Guy Fieri history. Walk down the historic main street, and take a trip back to the 1880s.

How to get to Ferndale:

Ferndale is 100 miles south of the Oregon border off Hwy. 101.

Pioneer Grave

O n a road trip, some of the most important discoveries are
unplanned. One day while driving along California Highway
20 in the glorious sunshine, I happened upon a small grave next

to the road. It was the tiny grave of a young pioneer, Julius Albert Apperson.

The ***Apperson family*** were early pioneers crossing the Sierra Nevada Mountains on a four month journey starting in Independence, Missouri. They decided to stay just outside Nevada City, California and homestead there. On May 6, 1858, the four Apperson children were outside burning debris when the youngest, 2-year old Julius' pant leg caught fire. He suffered severe burns and spent the next month fighting for his life, but he eventually died. He is buried in a small grave surrounded by a white picket fence just off the highway. His grave marker reads *"Julius Albert Apperson, born June 1855. Died May 6 1858. A pioneer who crossed*

the plain to California who died and was buried here." I will remember this little guy whenever I start to think my life is tough. Godspeed Julius.

How to get to the grave of Julius Albert Apperson:

The small grave is located just off California Hwy. 20 near Nevada City, California

Donner Memorial

T he ***Donner Memorial*** is a somber place, in sharp contrast
to the spectacular surroundings of Donner Lake and the
majestic Sierra Nevada Mountains. The memorial is dedicated

to the Donner Party, many of whom lost their lives at the spot near Donner Lake, on their way to a better life in California. As I explored the woods at the Donner Memorial, I felt grateful to not have been a pioneer. You walk a path that meanders gently through the woods, past markers to commemorate events of the tragedy. There is nothing left of the camps.

There is a separate historical site about 6 miles from the Donner Memorial. The park ranger at the Visitors Center can tell you how to get there. It is an absolute must-see because it is the actual site of the Donner camp after they became separated from the main party that camped at the lake.

It is a short hiking loop with markers detailing life at the Donner camp. It's a beautiful spot, making it hard to imagine the devastating winter the Donner party spent there. The excellent Visitor's Center has some interesting artifacts, including a hunting rifle belonging to a member of the party.

There is still a lot of controversy about whether the Donner party members actually resorted to cannibalism. As of now, there is no archaeological evidence that it happened. During excavations, only bear, deer and other wild animal bones have been found which show evidence of being eaten.

The name Sierra Nevada was first spoken by a Spanish missionary in 1772, meaning snow-capped mountains. In fact, snow falls in the Sierras in record amounts. In 1880, Southern Pacific railroad crews recorded a depth at Donner Pass of 31 feet. They also recorded a 68 foot total snowfall for the winter of 1938. It is this treacherous area that claimed the lives of many of the Donner Party. CSP, Rarick

How to get to the Donner Memorial:

The Donner Memorial is located near Truckee, California at 12593 Donner Pass Road.

A moment in time:

On April 15, 1846, farmers George and Jacob Donner, and their friend, cabinetmaker James Reed, left Springfield, Illinois with 9 wagons and headed west. They carried Lansford Hastings's book "The Emigrants' Guide to Oregon and California." The Breen and Murphy families, and several others left Independence, Missouri, headed for California. They were a small part of a massive wagon train.

Midway through the journey, the Donner contingent decided to try a new route, a cut-off touted by a man named Lansford Hastings. The Hastings cut-off, just outside of Fort Bridger, Wyoming, was supposed to cut both time and miles from the trip. The only problem was, Hastings had never traveled the route. ^{Wagner}

The disastrous decision to take the Hastings cut-off resulted in the party traversing nearly impassable terrain. They reached the Sierra Nevada Mountains, unable to cross them before winter set in. The Donner party reached Alder Creek to spend the winter. The Breen, Graves, Reed, and Murphy families made it to Truckee Lake, later named Donner lake. James Reed, the patriarch of the Reed family, was banished from the group earlier, for killing a man while he was in a fit of rage. He would later play a vital role in saving members of the group, including his family.

Thus began a hardship difficult to imagine. The members of the party ate their remaining stores of food as the snow piled up around them. Next, the remaining oxen were eaten, followed by any family dogs that had made it through. Animal hides were boiled down, cut into strips, and eaten. As food supplies were exhausted, the trapped emigrants decided to cannibalize family members and friends who had already died, as a final attempt to survive.

Four separate rescue parties were sent out to retrieve the surviving members of the Donner party. In mid-December, the first group of able-bodied men and women left camp to make their way across the mountains. Out of the group of 15, only 7 made it through to Bear Valley, on the way to Sutter's Fort. Tamsen Donner stayed behind to care for her dying husband, but sent her daughters off with the third rescue party.

Five weeks later, the final rescue party reached the cabins, and only one man was left. Louis Keseberg, a German immigrant, was still alive, but Tamsen Donner's body was never found. Louis Keseberg joked about cannibalizing her body, and he was taunted as a man-eater for the rest of his life.

81 people were trapped in the mountains, more than half of which were under 18, and a quarter of them were age 5 or younger, with 6 babies. Of the 81 people stranded in the mountains, 36 were dead, and 45 lived through the ordeal. The final rescue party came down from the mountains in April of 1847. Reason Tucker, a member of the first and the last rescue parties, described the mountain camps as having bones scattered about and skulls opened up to eat the brains. He described it as a place of "Death & Destruction." Rarick

Voices from the past:

"I never could have believed we could have traveled so far with so little difficulty." **From a letter written by Tamzene Donner, when she was near the junction of the North and South Platte Rivers, in Nebraska, June 16, 1846.**

"When I was forced to part with him, I cried until I was ill, and sat in the back of the wagon watching him become smaller and smaller as we drove on, until I could see him no more." Virginia Reed, on abandoning Billy, her pony, who could no longer continue on the exhausting journey to California. Rarick

Sunday 29th of Nov... *"Still snowing now about 3 feet deep, hard to get wood"* Monday 30th... *"No living thing without wings can get about"* By Sunday Dec 13th he writes... *"snow 8 feet deep on the level"* Monday Dec 21... *"Jake Donno Sam Shoemaker, Rinehart & Smith are dead. Wed Dec 30... 'Charley died last night Friday Feb 5th... "Eddy's child died last night", Monday Feb 8th...-Spitzer died last night...we will bury him in the snow"* Friday Feb 12th... *"We hope with the assistance of Almighty God to be able to live to see the bare surface of the earth once more"* Friday Feb 26th... *"Mrs. Murphy said here yesterday that thought she would commence on Milt and eat him. It is distressing."* **From the diary of Patrick Breen**. ^{Teggart}

Marshall Gold Discovery

The **Marshall Gold Discovery State Historic Park** is the site of **Sutter's Mill**, where James Marshall and John Sutter found gold in 1848. The California gold rush started out here and it's a must see. It's also the site of **Coloma**, the original gold rush town, with buildings dating from the 1850s. In 1847 Sutter commissioned James Marshall to build a sawmill on the American River. On Jan. 24, 1848 Marshall found a gold nugget in the mill tailings, bringing about the gold rush of 1849. Miners flooded in, confiscating most of Sutter's property.

The town name of Coloma is derived from the original Nisenan Indian name of Kullomah. [Bottjer] When I walked around the wonderful old town, a group of deer followed me wherever I went. My favorite building is the jail, which was built in 1857, because the original jail was built of logs, and the second jail, built in 1855, was too small.

Another fascinating building is the Wah Hop Chinese Store, built in the 1850s.

Don't miss the pioneer cemetery, where many of the 49ers gold seekers are spending eternity. This was also the site of a double hanging of convicted murderers in 1855. The Visitor's Center at Marshall Gold Discovery holds an interesting collection of artifacts, including a stagecoach from the 1850s, gaming pieces, an old doll, and a wine bottle from 1872 which was found in the remains of a building. California State Parks

How to get to Marshall Gold Discovery State Historic Park:

Marshall Gold Discovery State Historic Park is located in the town of Coloma at 310 Back Street.

Profiles in history:

James Marshall, the founder of the California Gold Rush, was born on October 8, 1810, in New Jersey. He discovered gold on the American River, near the town of Coloma, on January 24, 1848. Marshall was commissioned to build a mill on the property by Johann Sutter. Marshall built the mill, but the gold find resulted in no one working the mill, so the mill floundered and eventually went to ruin. Marshall was forced off the land by an influx of prospectors. After various unsuccessful ventures including a vineyard, and investment in another gold mine, Marshall was granted a two-year pension by the State of California. The pension was renewed twice but then eventually stopped in 1878. Marshall died in poverty on August 10, 1885. [Enss]

Voices from the past:

"...I then collected four or five pieces and went up to Mr. Scott with the pieces in my hand and said, "I have found it." "What is it?" inquired Scott. "Gold," I answered. "Oh! No," replied Scott, "That can't be." I said, "I know it to be nothing else." **James Marshall, on finding gold in the American River, 1848.**

Sacramento

Old Sacramento is a charming place to spend a few hours. Many of the historic buildings date from the time of the Gold Rush in the 1850's. This area of town is filled with unique shops and casual eateries which make it a blissful little walk through time.

Old town Sacramento lies right next to the river, which adds to the ambience. As you stroll through town, don't miss the statue dedicated to Pony Express Riders. Stop in at the ***Sacramento History Museum***, which contains a fascinating collection of artifacts and historical photos. There are also some very large gold nuggets to enjoy.

Sutter's Fort in downtown Sacramento, was built by Johann Augustus Sutter in 1840. Sutter was granted 150,000 acres of land by the Mexican government, and established a fort with thick adobe walls, massive gates and cannons for defense against Indian attacks. The fort supplied food, supplies and shelter to settlers coming to California. The employees of Sutter helped to rescue the Donner party in 1847.

How to get to Sacramento historic sites:

The Sacramento History Museum is located at 101 "I" Street

Sutter's Fort is located in Sacramento at 2701 L Street

Profiles in history:

Johann Augustus Sutter was born in 1803 in Germany. He left Europe in 1834, leaving his wife and kids because of debts he owed. He swindled and borrowed his way to California in 1839, where he was commissioned to build the fort, which now lies in downtown Sacramento.

Sutter became a citizen of Mexico in 1840 in order to build the fort on the land. Through the Mexican government, he acquired more land so eventually he controlled almost 300 square miles between Sacramento and Redding. He sold the fort for $7000 when his family came to California in 1849. Sutter wore many hats during his lifetime, including that of a swindler, soldier, patriot, and debtor. Throughout his life he had problems with money, so he spent his old age near poverty. He died in Pennsylvania in 1880 and his funeral was attended by Mark Twain, General Phil Sheridan, and explorer John C. Fremont, who gave the eulogy. Enss

Ghost story:

Many sick and injured were treated at Sutter's Fort, and those who died of injuries, cholera, yellow fever, and typhoid were buried quickly nearby, often with no grave marker. One such burial was found when a sewer was put in. Artifacts found with the remains date to the late 1840s. Spiritually sensitive people feel a strong sense of misery both inside and outside the fort. Dwyer

Fort Ross

*F*ort Ross founded in 1812, is North America's southernmost
Russian settlement. The Russian-American Company manager, Alexander Baranov, entrusted his assistant, Ivan Kuskov, to

find a site in California to locate the settlement. Kuskov arrived by ship in 1809. Fur traders who were members of the Russian-American Company built the settlement. The settlement was named "Ross" to honor their homeland of Russia.

In 1812, Kuskov led 25 Russians and 80 Alaskans to build structures and defensive walls. Fort Ross had 41 cannons for defense and were able to repel skirmishes against the Spanish. The blockhouses were equipped with a flagstaff, to provide warnings in case of attacks and to help guide ships approaching the fort.

As you walk the grounds, you can see the ***Kuskov House***, the massive building next to the chapel. The upstairs of the building functioned as living quarters for the first administrator, Ivan Kuskov, and his family. The downstairs of the building functioned as an armory, containing muskets, powder, and other weapons.

You can also see the ***Rotchev House***, built in 1836, where Alexander Rotchev the last manager of the Ross settlement lived with his wife, Yelena, and their three children. It is the only original structure from the settlement. The house contained a library, piano forte, and fine French wines.

The **chapel** was built in the mid 1820s. Unfortunately, the chapel had no priest in residence. In 1836, Father Ioann Veniaminov, visited the chapel, and wrote in his journal, " the chapel at Fort Ross receives almost no income from its members or from those Russians who are occasional visitors."

You can also see workshops, a supply house, a fur warehouse, and barracks within the walls of the fort.The various talents of the settlement inhabitants are on display, including woodworking, blacksmithing, barrel making, and shipbuilding. The first ship constructed in California was the Rumiantsev, built in 1818. Fort Ross was sold to John Sutter, owner of Sutter's Fort, in 1841. [CSP]

How to get to Fort Ross:

Fort Ross is located 11 miles northwest of Jenner on Hwy. 1

Voices from the past:

"*...What an enchanting land California is!...the vegetation is in full bloom and everything is so fragrant. The iridescent hummingbird flutters, vibrates and shimmers like a precious stone on the branch or over a flower. The virgin soil of California yields marvelous fruits...I spent the best years of my life there, and affectionately carry the memories of these days in my soul...*" ***Alexander Rotchev***

Sonoma State
Historic Park

T he **Sonoma State Historic Park** covers several locations and contains numerous historic buildings. The **Mission San Francisco de Solano** is the northernmost of the Spanish Missions in California and the last mission to be established. The site was consecrated on July 4, 1823, and a small wooden church was built in 1824. The mission became individual parishes in 1834, and began a collapse which ended in the late 1830s.

The **Sonoma Barracks** housed General Vallejo's army beginning in 1834. Later, Vallejo remodeled the building to serve as a winery. Inside you can see a copy of the California bear flag. The red stripe at the bottom is said to come from a petticoat. CSP

The ***Toscano Hotel*** which began as the Hotel Eureka, was built in the 1850s and was home to a retail store and library. The hotel was bought by an Italian family who changed the name in the 1890s. A separate building houses the kitchen and dining room. The ***Blue Wing Inn*** was built to house soldiers at the Sonoma mission. Actress Lotta Crabtree and Army officer Ulysses S. Grant both stayed at the inn. At this time, you can't go inside the inn due to unsafe conditions.

The Sonoma State Historic Park is also the site of the first flying of California's bear flag on June 14, 1846. Americans proclaimed California as independent of Mexico in what was known as the Bear Flag Revolt. A small boulder and plaque in the lovely park across the street commemorate the event.

Lachryma Montis, Vallejo's "American Style" home is in a separate location about ½ mile away from the other Sonoma historic buildings. The building was prefabricated and shipped to Sonoma around Cape Horn. The long building known as the ***Chalet*** was also prefabricated, and was originally a warehouse for wine and produce. Now it is the park museum.

How to get to Sonoma State Historic Park:

The park is located at 363 Third Street West in Sonoma, California.

Profiles in history:

Mariano Guadalupe Vallejo was born on July 4, 1807, and was
the eighth of thirteen children. He was an accomplished man,
speaking Spanish, English, French, and Latin. In 1834, Vallejo stole
prized grape vines from the Mission San Francisco Solano. These
grape vines were replanted onto Vallejo's property, allowing Vallejo to become one of the first winegrowers in California. Vallejo
became Commandant General of Alta California at the age of
29. He became a statesman who was instrumental in California
becoming part of the United States, having supported American
immigration into the area, rather than submitting to British or
French rule. Mariano Guadalupe Vallejo died on January 18, 1890,
at his home, Lachryma Montis. He was chosen to be immortalized
at the National Hall of Statuary in Washington, D. C. Lachryma
Montis means tears of the mountains.

A word about the California Bear Flag:

In June, 1846, the famous California Bear Flag was made in the Sonoma Barracks. The flag flew over Sonoma until July 9th, to be replaced by the Stars and Stripes. The flag in Sonoma is a copy made by the Society of California Pioneers.

Voices from the past:

"The flag was made in the front room of the barracks, just at the left of the door, and most of the sewing was done by myself. 'Bill' Todd painted the bear and star with black ink..." **Benjamin Dewell**

"...One of the ladies at the garrison gave us a piece of brown domestic, and Mrs. Captain John Sears gave us some strips of red flannel about four inches wide. The domestic was new, but the flannel was said to have been part of a petticoat worn by Mrs. Sears across the mountains..." **William L. 'Bill' Todd**

Mission San Francisco de Asis

M *ission San Francisco de Asis*, also known as Mission Dolores, is a place of peace and serenity. Mission Dolores is the sixth mission established under the leadership of Father Junipero Serra. The mission was established on October 9, 1776. The mission building is the oldest intact mission, and has walls 4 feet thick. The redwood roof timbers, which are lashed with rawhide, are original.

According to Father Cambon, who constructed Mission Dolores in 1788, 36,000 adobe bricks were needed in the construction of Mission Dolores. The church altar was created in San Blas, Mexico, and came to the mission in 1796. Above the altar is a statue of Mater Dolorosa, Our Lady of Sorrows.

The cemetery contains burials from the early days of the mission up until the 1890s. Some notable figures from history are buried here including including Lieutenant Jose Joaquin Moraga, who led the 1776 expedition into the area, Don Luis Antonio Arguello, the first governor of Alta California under Mexican rule, and Don Francisco de Haro, the first Alcalde of San Francisco.

How to get to Mission Dolores:

Mission Dolores is located at the intersection of 16th and Dolores Streets, in San Francisco, CA.

San Francisco

D riving across San Francisco's ***Golden Gate Bridge*** is an experience everyone should enjoy at least once. It's a monumental man-made achievement recognized throughout the world. Construction of the bridge began in 1933, and it was opened for public use in 1937. Deep in the waters beneath the bridge, the steamboat, *City of Chester*, lies undisturbed. It was sunk in August, 1890.

The ***Presidio*** is where San Francisco began. It was first used by the Spanish, from 1776 to 1821, then by Mexico, from 1822 to 1846, and then by the United States, from 1846 to 1994.

San Francisco Bay is one of the largest natural harbors in the world and needed to be protected back in the 1800s from Spanish incursion. In 1870, the U.S. army began construction on a system of gun batteries along the bluffs bordering the bay.

The famous ***Fisherman's Wharf*** began it's life in 1884, and has grown into one of the most popular tourist attractions in San Francisco. The many shops and eateries are a pleasant way to spend the day.

No tour of San Francisco would be complete without a trip out to Alcatraz Island, home of the infamous *Alcatraz prison*. The prison began incarcerating prisoners as early as 1859. Alcatraz prison once housed Confederate prisoners caught on the West Coast, Native Americans who would not send their children off to Indian boarding schools run by the American Government, and mobster Al Capone.

A moment in time:

San Francisco trembled and fell when an earthquake with an estimated magnitude of 7.9 rocked the Northern California coast. Fires soon engulfed San Francisco, destroying over 80% of the city, and killing over 3,000 people. Hundreds of thousands of people were left homeless and were living in tents in Golden Gate Park and the beaches for over two years. It was the deadliest earthquake in United States history.

Voices from the past:

" The street was a wall of flame. And against this wall of flame, sil-houetted sharply, were two United States cavalrymen sitting their horses, calmly watching. That was all. Not another person was in sight. In the intact heart of the city two troopers sat their horses and watched. Surrender was complete. There was no water." **Jack London, April 17, 1906.**

"Today is my birthday. Last night I was worth thirty thousand dollars. I bought five bottles of wine, some delicate fish, and other things for my birthday dinner. I have had no dinner, and all I own

are these crutches." **Disabled man speaking to Jack London,
April 17, 1906.**

*"Yesterday morning, I was worth six hundred thousand dollars.
This morning, this house is all I have left,. It will go in fifteen
minutes. This rug upon which we stand is a present. It cost fifteen
hundred dollars. Try that piano. Listen to its tone. There are few
like it. There are no horses. The flames will be here in fifteen
minutes."* **San Francisco citizen speaking to Jack London,
April 17, 1906.**

Fun fact:

The term "Golden Gate" was first spoken by famous explorer John Charles Fremont as he crossed San Francisco Bay.

Mission San Jose

Mission San Jose was founded on June 11, 1797, by Father Fermin de Lasuen. It became the fourteenth Spanish mission in California. It was founded on land inhabited by the

Ohlone people. The original structures were built with thatched roofs. A more permanent adobe church was built in 1809, but was destroyed in 1868 by a massive earthquake. In 1833, the missions, including Mission San Jose, became the property of the Mexican government. Mission lands were divided up into ranchos.

The interior of the mission church is restored to how it would have looked in 1833. The walls of the mission are between 4 and 5 feet thick.

The mission museum contains austere rooms, sparsely furnished with simple chairs, tables, and beds.

One of my favorite pieces in the museum is this harmonium. Originally invented in France about 1850, this harmonium may have been part of the original adobe church.

During excavations, the grave of Robert Livermore, an English-born, California ranchero in Alta California, was found under the church floor, along with the graves of many others who were buried without markers. Note the skull and crossbones design above the door. This symbol was used to signify a cemetery.

How to get to Mission San Jose:

Mission San Jose is located at 43300 Mission Blvd. in Fremont, California.

San Jose

S*an Jose* is the home of the ***Winchester Mystery House***. Sarah Winchester came to California in 1884, the widow of William Winchester, creator of the Winchester rifle. Through seances, Sarah's husband came to her with a message. She was to build a large mansion, big enough to hold the spirits of those killed by her husband's invention. The mansion was built by craftsmen working every hour of every day, 365 days a year. It was continuously remodeled at a cost of 5.5 million dollars. Work continued on until Sarah's death in 1922. Finch

How to get to Winchester Mystery House:

The Winchester Mystery House is located at 525 S Winchester Blvd, in San Jose.

Ghost story:

Sarah Winchester's ghost is said to inhabit the Winchester Mystery House, causing visitors to report breathing sounds, footsteps, and feelings of someone lightly touching their arms. There are also reports of a workman dressed in overalls appearing in the basement. He often pushes a wheelbarrow. [Mayo]

Bodie

*B*odie is one of the best ghost towns I've ever seen. The road to get there, however, is about like driving on a washboard for 20 miles. It's bumpy, but so worth it, once you get there. You can pick up a walking map and history of Bodie at the Visitor's Center.

You can walk freely around the entire town of about 200 buildings. Amazingly, the 200 buildings still standing represent only about 5% of the total buildings during Bodie's peak years of 1877 to 1881. Bodie is the largest unrestored ghost town in the United States.

Bodie began its life when gold was discovered in 1859 by W.S. Bodey. He died in a blizzard months later, never able to see the town with his name. His bones were found in 1879 and then reburied. The location is uncertain, but is rumored to be on the hill above the town cemetery. CSP, Geissinger

At its peak, Bodie had close to 10,000 residents with 30 mines, and over 60 saloons, and it became the third largest city in California. By 1880, there were about 2000 buildings in Bodie.

Bodie residents enjoyed a roller skating rink, bowling alley, race-track, and a baseball league, along with dancing, gambling, and a red-light district. Winter holidays were spent indoors, due to high snow drifts, which once reached as high as 28 feet. Fourth of July was an important holiday for Bodie. Residents spent four to six days enjoying Independence Day, with a lively parade going down main street.

As you walk around town, look for the Old Methodist Church, built in 1882, by Rev. F.M. Warrington. There are so many wonderful structures including the Wheaton & Luhrs Store, built in the early 1880s, the morgue, and the jail.

You can also see the Cain Residence, known as the finest house in Bodie, built in 1879. It was the home of James Stuart Cain, from one of Bodie's most important families, and his wife Delilah. They lived in the house up until the 1940s.

Many Bodie residents couldn't afford fine houses, so they would live in common houses like this one, costing about $300. Geissinger

Also look for the site of Thomas Treloar's murder. He was shot and killed January 14, 1881 by Joseph DeRoche, who was involved with Treloar's wife. DeRoche escaped, but was apprehended and brought back to the Bodie jail. Vigilantes took him from his cell and hanged him at the site.

Guests at one of main hotels in town, the Occidental, dined on white linen tablecloths, with fine china and crystal. Fresh fruit accompanied each meal, and for dessert, there was a choice between pie and cake. Giessinger

Miners in Bodie had a rough life. They worked 12 hour days, 6 days per week, and were paid a mere 4 dollars per day. In the winter, many miners would spend their nights sitting in chairs in the saloons, which were heated, rather than going to their freezing cold beds. Pneumonia was the most common killer of Bodie residents, miners, and non-miners alike. ^{Giessinger}

How to get to Bodie:

Bodie ghost town is near the town of Bridgeport, close to the Nevada border. The road to get there is rough and unpaved, so be careful.

A word about the Bodie Cemetery:

The Bodie Pioneer Cemetery was founded in 1859. Thomas Tre-loar is buried there. He was murdered by his wife's lover, Joseph DeRoche, who was later apprehended and hung outside of town.

A woman named Mary Turner is also buried there. Mary was 19 years old when she died, and her body was later exhumed by a Bodie doctor named Blackwood and dissected. When the doctor was finished, he dropped her body down into a mine shaft. Blackwood kept Mary's skull in his office. Blackwood fled Bodie and was never brought to justice.

Another occupant of Bodie Pioneer Cemetery is a little girl, whose grave is marked by a marble angel. This is the grave of Evelyn Myers, a three-year-old girl. Evelyn loved to follow a local miner around. She crept behind him one day as he was raising his pickax to begin chipping rock. The pickax hit poor Evelyn, killing her. Her gravestone reads *"Beloved Daughter."* [Enss]

Profiles in history:

Eleanora Dumont was born in 1829 and became one of the most successful gamblers in the West. She opened the Dumont House in Nevada City in 1854. She equipped Dumont House with fine furnishings and the finest liquor. Eleanora Dumont was beautiful, but unsuccessful at love. She was swindled and cheated by a variety of men. As Eleanora aged, she began to grow hair on her upper lip, and came to be known as "Madame Moustache." She met and married a man named Jack McNight, and they moved to Carson, Nevada, and bought a ranch. Her life was happy for awhile, until she woke up one morning and found there was no Jack. He had taken all of her jewelry and money and skipped town. Stories spread that Madame Moustache tracked down McNight and killed him. She went back to the gambling tables, first in San Francisco, and later in Bodie, California. She died in Bodie in 1879, down on her luck once again. Madame Moustache committed suicide by taking poison.

Columbia State Historic Park

*C*olumbia State Historic Park contains the town of Columbia, which began its life on March 27, 1850. Gold was found there by a group of prospectors who were "drying out" during a rainstorm. By 1852, Columbia had over 150 businesses in town, including stores and saloons. Columbia also had three churches and a Masonic Lodge.

In 1853, the town of Columbia became one of the largest cities in California. 150 million dollars in gold was mined in Columbia. Columbia State Historic Park contains what is the largest collection of structures from the days of the Gold Rush.[CSP]

One of my favorite buildings was the dentist office, which offered a complete set-up of frightening instruments used in the 1850s and 1860s.

Other fascinating buildings include the Wells Fargo building, Chinese store, drugstore, and the stone jail.

How to get to Columbia State Historic Park:

Columbia State Historic Park is in Columbia, California.

Ghost story:

The City Hotel, now a part of Columbia State Historic Park, was built in 1856. It didn't start out haunted. An antique bed was brought over from the Midwest in the 1870s by a gentleman trying to make his fortune. He eventually sent for his wife, but she died on her way to California. The bed was passed among many antique dealers, but eventually was brought back to the City Hotel in Columbia, California. Guests of the hotel have reported mournful sobbing, rose scented perfume, cold spots, and door rattling when they sleep in the bed. It is believed that a woman died in childbirth in room #1 that housed the bed. Dwyer

Voices from the past:

"I once traveled with a party of New Yorkers en route for California... They soon learned that champagne, East India sweetmeats, olives, etc. etc., were not the most useful articles for a prairie tour." **from The Prairie Traveler by Randolph Marcy, Captain U .S. Army, 1859.**

A word about mules:

Mules were often used instead of horses because they were stronger and could endure the hardships of scarce water and food. They recovered more quickly from periods of fasting, and their hooves could withstand unstable terrain better than horses. A single mule would commonly be hitched up to a 2000 pound load of ore. Mules were well cared for, with a veterinarian always on hand to treat sick or injured mules. Small injuries were treated underground in the mines, but for larger injuries or serious illnesses, mules were moved to the surface. Giessinger

Mission San Juan Bautista

*M*ission San Juan Bautista was founded June 24, 1797, by Father Fermin de Lasuen, and completed by Father Felipe Arroyo de la Cuesta, becoming the fifteenth Spanish mission in California. San Juan Bautista has the only original Spanish plaza in California.The church was built in 1803, and it is the widest of the mission churches. The church was dedicated in 1812.

The altar within the church was painted by Thomas Doak in 1818. Doak was a sailor originally from Boston, who deserted in Monterey. He came to the mission and completed the altar as payment for room and board.

Father Esteban Tapis, an incomparable musical talent, brought his talents with him to San Juan Bautista. Two of his handwritten choir books are in the museum. The mission became known as the "Mission of Music." Father Tapis is buried in the church.

The gift shop was once a storehouse. In 1847, the Breen family, who survived the Donner tragedy, lived in the storehouse. The Breen family bible is in the mission museum.

The cemetery is said to contain over 4300 burials dating from 1808 to the 1930s.

A word about the California Missions:

During the years 1769 to 1833 Franciscan priests established a network of 21 Spanish missions, stretching from San Diego to San Francisco, a distance of 600 miles. The function of the Spanish missions was to bring Christianity to the indigenous peoples, and to protect Spanish interests in what was known as Alta California.

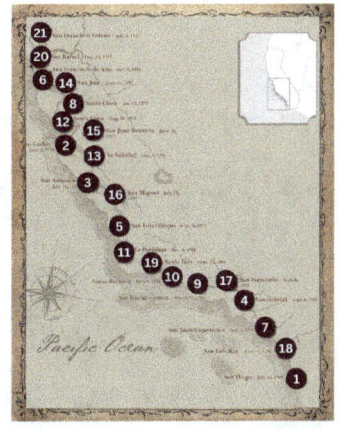

18 of the 21 missions were founded by Father Junipero Serra, and Father Fermin de Lasuen, both of whom are buried at Carmel Mission. Other priests involved in the founding of the missions were Father Jose Ramon Abella, Father Jose Altimira, Father Pedro Benito Cambon, Father Estevan Tapis, Father Luis Gil y Taboada, Father Vicente Francisco de Sarria, and Father Narciso Duran.

Monterey

*M**onterey*** is a beautiful city, on the spectacular California coast. John Steinbeck wrote about it, and now you can visit its famous Cannery Row for yourself.

The *Fisherman's Wharf*, one of Monterey's main attractions, was built out of stone in 1846, and then rebuilt in the early 1900's when commercial fishing became an industry. As you stroll the wharf, don't miss the wonderful carved wooden statues everywhere.

When in Monterey, an absolute must-see is the world famous ***Monterey Bay Aquarium***. My favorites are the clownfish and blue tangs, but the jellyfish are pretty great too.

How to get to Monterey attractions:

The Fisherman's Wharf is located at #1 Old Fisherman's Wharf.

The Monterey Bay Aquarium is located at 886 Cannery Row.

Carmel Mission

T he ***Mission San Carlos Borromeo de Carmelo***, also
known as the Carmel Mission, is an amazing place. The

mission was founded in 1771 by Father Junipero Serra. It's the only mission that retains its original bell and tower.

Early Spanish history is alive here, in the many furnished rooms that look like they were vacated just yesterday.

The mission also contains the first library of California with books brought by the Franciscan missionaries. Pope John Paul II visited the mission in 1987.

Don't miss the Convento Museum, which has the cell used by Saint Junipero Serra and where he died in 1784. Carmel Mission

How to get to Carmel Mission:

Carmel Mission is in the city of Carmel-by-the-Sea at 3080 Rio Road.

Profiles in history:

Father Junipero Serra founded 9 of the 21 California missions. He was born in 1713 on the island of Majorca, and became a Franciscan at the age of 16. On his ordainment, he changed his name to Junipero, which means "Jester of God." Serra was a small man, about 5 feet 2 inches tall, with a serious demeanor. While walking 270 miles to Mexico City, Serra was bit by a mosquito and the bite became infected. His leg and his health would never be the same. He would travel some 24,000 miles over the course of his life, going up and down the coast of California, searching for more mission locations.

Father Serra wasn't afraid to suffer and endure martyrdom to expand the missions. He used various methods of self-torment including wearing hair shirts, whipping himself, and holding candles to his body to punish his own unworthiness. He died in 1874

at Carmel Mission and is buried next to the altar in the Mission
Church.

A word about mission life for Indians:

In 1786, French ships visited Monterey and the Carmel Mission. They brought Jean Francois de la Perouse along with scientists, physicians, and cartographers. Perouse made a written record of what he found at the Carmel Mission. These are some of the observations:

The listing of the number of souls saved in 10 missions from San Diego to San Carlos, dated 1769 to 1786, is a total of 5143 Indians. After baptism, the Indians had to work at least 7 hours each day, and remained in prayer for 2 hours. They could not escape to their family living elsewhere because soldiers were dispatched to bring them back and whip them.

Many children died of hernias. Indians butchered cows and ate the meat raw suggesting extreme hunger. Some Indians wore leg irons and were whipped. Women were whipped in private; men were whipped in full view of everyone as a deterrent.

From The Journals of La Perouse, life in a California mission Margolin

Voices from the past:

"I have never seen one laugh...they look as though they were interested in nothing." **Louis Choris, a member of the La Perouse party.**

"All operations and functions both of body and mind appeared to be carried out with a mechanical, lifeless, careless indifference." **Captain Vancouver** Margolin

Soledad Mission

The ***Soledad Mission*** was founded in 1791 by Father Fermin de Lasuen and is the thirteenth of the Spanish Missions in California.

The mission museum contains several rooms, separated by time period. One of the my favorite pieces in the museum is this original mission bell, cast in Mexico in 1799. The Mission Room is dedicated to the original founding of the mission, and up to the 1830s. There are several interesting fragments of sandals.

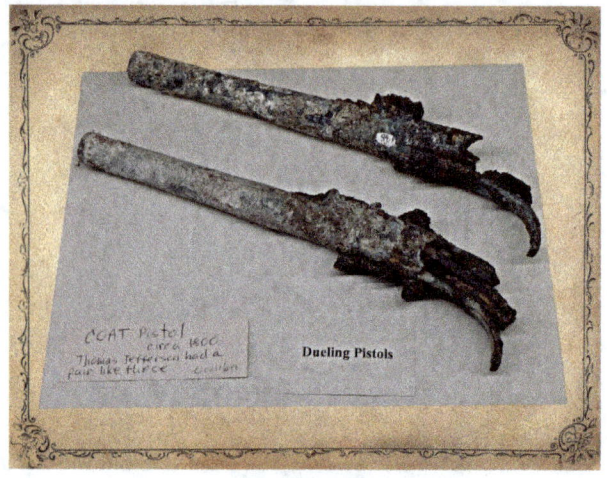

COAT Pistol
circa 1800.
Thomas Jefferson had a
pair like these   double
Dueling Pistols

The Rancho Room contains artifacts dating from when the mission became the property of the Mexican government, including these coat pistols. The mission was sold to the Soberanes family for $800.

As you walk the grounds, you will notice what is left of the Quad-rangle, containing the original adobe rooms where the work of the mission took place.

The Chapel contains an altar with a statue of Our Lady of Sorrows. The paintings and wood carvings of the river of life, are said to represent souls bobbing up and down. Arrows on the ceiling point to heaven.

Father Florencio Ibanez, who died in 1818, is the only priest buried at the mission. He taught music and loved putting on a nativity play.

How to get to Soledad Mission:

Soledad Mission is located at 36641 Fort Romie Rd, Soledad, CA.

Favorite Places to Camp

The ***Nevada County Fairgrounds*** is one of the loveliest places I have ever stayed. The campground has everything, a fishing pond, tall pine trees, and expansive sites, along with showers, and plenty of places to walk a dog. It's a perfect home base to explore Nevada City, Placerville, and other parts of the gold country. Register online at ***https://nevadacountyfair.com/rv-park***

Camping in the ***Redwoods*** simply can't be beat, and there are many campgrounds and dispersed camping available. For more information, visit ***https://www.visitredwoods.com/explore-the-redwoods/camping-in-the-redwoods***

Random Thoughts
What History Means to Me

First, let me start by sharing with you my opinion of what history isn't. History is not a collection of random dates, names, and places for you to memorize. History is not a dry and uninteresting class you have to pass to graduate.

I believe history is a tangible thing. You can actually *feel* history in the places you go, and the sights you see. I remember walking up to the Acropolis in Athens. I looked down at the well-worn marble steps and wondered about how many ancient philosophers had climbed these very steps, thousands of years ago.

You don't have to go far away to experience the *feeling* of history. If you are lucky enough to live in an old house, you may experience history in your own surroundings. You might say to yourself, *"If only these walls could talk."*

During my travels across the United States, I *felt* history in many, many places. If you travel across the country like I did, you will *feel* the wonderful history of our beautiful country for yourself, and you will never be the same. You will discover what it means to be an American.

Why I did it and why you can too:

I decided to travel across the country by car because I wanted to rediscover America. When I first set out to explore the history of our country, I wanted to find out why America is the greatest country on earth, and what it means to be an American.

The politics of these United States was frightening at the time. Our country was polarized, almost beyond repair. Whether it was Democrats or Republicans, Conservatives, or Liberals, everyone was fighting.

I wanted to rediscover the joy of being an American. I wanted to rediscover our rich history, our unique and wonderful people, our tapestry of multicultural heritage, and our rich natural resources. I thought a road trip by car across eleven western states was a good place to start.

I have a degree in Archaeology, and a passion for all things archaeological. I love history, with a side love of paleontology. It is these three passions that I set my trip agenda around. I set out to discover the archaeological sites, history, and paleontological world of our country.

As I travel and write my books, I get asked all the time, especially by women, "What is it like to travel by yourself? Aren't you scared?" The truth is, I believe everyone should do what I did. It's a wonderful way to discover our country, and to rediscover yourself. The truth is, I'm scared not to travel. Traveling allows you to get to know yourself, in ways not possible when sitting on the couch watching TV.

We tend to spend a lot of our lives tuning out the world and our place within it. When you travel, you are quite literally forced to deal with your own thoughts, emotions, and feelings. You can discover yourself while traveling. You can come to understand what makes you who you are, and how you can perhaps become a better person. Above all, traveling gives you mental clarity to figure out how to live with intent. It's a way to guide your life, not just wait for things to happen.

Travel Tips & Stuff

What You Need to Know

How to get started:

P lanning your trip should be one of the most exciting things about it. You want to be spontaneous, but it is also very wise to plan your route, so you can take full advantage of all the time and miles you will invest.

- First, decide your passions. If you love airplanes, trains, or old vehicles, plan your trip around that. If you love gardens or architecture, seek that out as the focus of your trip.

- Next, read and research areas of the country that will let you enjoy what you are interested in.

- Make a list by state and city or town, of what you want to see.

- Take your handy road atlas and locate the areas on the pages.

- Make a tentative route plan, so you have an idea of where you are going.

Travel tip: Avoid trying to plan your trip down to a schedule of days, hours, or minutes. On a road trip, it will be virtually impossible to know where you will be on any given day. If you adhere to a schedule, you are more likely to stress out, and less likely to actually enjoy yourself, which is the whole point.

What you need:

You need to bring along a sense of adventure and a curious mind. You need to ditch the idea of always being on a schedule, and live a little more spontaneously to thoroughly enjoy yourself. Things will happen as you travel, both good things and bad things, and you need to prepare your mind and your soul for day-to-day changes.

So much of our lives are planned out. Between growing up, going to school, finding a career, marriage, kids, or whatever, people have lost much of the ability to be spontaneous. But you must take spontaneity on the trip with you, because you may make detours along the way to see something really spectacular.

So, for the practical stuff you need:

A great vehicle-I have a Honda CRV which is fabulous. It's old, a 2004, fully paid for, and will go anywhere. I see humongous RVs on the road, towing a car behind, and all I can think of is, they can't go just anywhere. They are too big. Bad gas mileage, cumbersome to drive, slow, and not agile like my CRV. So, I encourage you, if you want to go car camping and be able to go on remote dirt roads, get an agile vehicle, and Hondas are great.

Travel tip: Don't be afraid to do some modifications to your vehicle. I took one of my back seats out. (after watching a YouTube video) I threw in a twin mattress, a bit of drapery, and some netting. I also put some of those little portable light switches on the inside. I jettisoned anything I hadn't used up to that point. Don't be afraid to get rid of unnecessary stuff.

An awesome camera that you know inside and out. I use a Nikon and it takes wonderful pictures. Don't skimp on a camera, and don't think a cellphone camera is all you need, because you want the best for your beautiful photos.

A hot plate warmer-this little item was indispensable. You need a converter for it so you can plug it in to the cigarette lighter. Place your food inside it, carton and all, and then plug it in. 30 minutes for thawed food, about an hour and a half for frozen food. Boom! You have a hot meal by the time you stop for the night!

Window shades-the best ones are magnetic so you just place them against your windows and they cling to them, obscuring the view inside your car.

Portable cooler with wheels-another indispensable item that works great and is easy to move around. I use those nifty blue frozen blocks in mine.

Portable air compressor-this little gem plugs into your cigarette lighter and will inflate your tires if you have a flat. Fortunately, I haven't had to use this yet.

Portable battery charger and power bank-mine comes with battery cables and the power bank, yet once inside the case, it is small enough to put in your glove compartment. This little item, unfortunately, I have had to use, and it saved me.

Portable generator-mine came with a small solar panel, so it can be charged with solar or electricity. It has a decent battery life and also doubles as a light for night-time.

All season clothing-you never know what different states will bring for weather, so take hot weather and cold weather clothes, and a fair amount of shoes appropriate for hiking, or walking, sandals, and slippers, which are nice at night. Also take along a pair of cheap rubber flip-flops to wear in the public showers you might go into.

Your own pillows-I like my own pillows, so I don't wake up with neck cramps, especially after sleeping in the car.

Sleeping bag and cozy blankets-you want to stay warm and layering is everything.

Warm hat, warm socks, and fuzzy jammies to keep you warm for cold nights sleeping in the car.

A great road atlas, and great guidebooks-get one that's easy to read, with great pictures. For a road atlas, just get one that is easy to read.

A word about photography:

Along with a great camera, you need to have a great eye. This is easier than it sounds once you have worked with your camera and are comfortable taking pictures with it. I am not a professional photographer, but I like my pictures and other people do too.

These are my tips for taking great pictures:

- Experiment with taking both horizontal and vertical shots.

- Don't always put the subject of the photo in the middle of the photograph.

- This one is important: pay attention to the foreground,

and if possible, have something, a plant or whatever, in the foreground to help give the photo dimension and depth.

- This one is important too: turn around often to see the view you just came from. I do this quite often and some of my best pictures have resulted from when I turned around and took the shot.

You can also take a mental photo. Place an image in your mind that you can call upon later. Use all of your senses to see, hear, smell, and maybe even to taste, what is around you. You have the means to fully experience your surroundings, and that is very important to a traveler. When you take a mental photo, be sure to jot down quick little details about what you saw, heard, smelled, or tasted, so you can jog your memory later.

And last, but not least...don't be posing in front of everything, everywhere, to show that you actually went somewhere. Most people want to see themselves in your photo and be mentally transported there, but they can't if you are there already.

To camp or not to camp:

Car camping is great. I prefer it to sleeping on the cold, hard ground in a tent. I can lock the doors, put my window shades up and be cozy for the night.

That being said, for me there were some do's and don'ts about camp sites. Some people camp in a Walmart parking lot and feel safe. I do not. I believe that if you are in a busy area, you're more likely to be confronted by a nut job who may bother you. Nothing against Walmart.

Same goes for casino parking lots. Many people believe that if they are in a public place, there is less chance of someone bothering them. I don't share this belief. I believe you are safer parked out in the middle of nowhere in the dark. That same nut job who can find you in a parking lot is not about to go driving around on dirt roads to see if anyone is parked there. At least that's my belief. You may not share it, and that's fine. Park and camp wherever you feel safe.

I don't go for rest areas either because they have a track record of incidents happening to people in rest areas, especially women travelers.

So, where do I camp? In state or national campgrounds, wildlife sanctuaries, or off on a dirt road somewhere, usually out in the middle of nowhere.

There are definitely times when I stay in a motel. I use Hotels.com because I like their stay 10 nights, get 1 night free deal. So, I book a hotel or motel if:

- The weather is too hot or too cold, or too rainy

- I am in a city and plan to stay awhile

- I'm tired of camping, need a shower, or my body hurts

- I need to do laundry

A word about safety:

When you are a woman traveling alone, it's critical to keep a low profile. Don't tell people you are traveling alone, where you are staying, or any other personal information.

I don't go to bars or get drunk. I'm not preaching but you are on your own, in a city or town you've never been to, and you don't know anyone, so it's not the time to lose control of what you are doing. When you are in control, you are better able to decide which people you want to get to know better.

Travel tip: If you feel vulnerable traveling alone, that's OK. Vulnerability is part of passion, and traveling is a passionate thing to do. You can put one of those family stickers on your vehicle to indicate to others that you are not traveling alone, which can help you feel more secure.

Maintain your connections:

When you are traveling alone, there is a definite sense of disconnection. It feels almost like you are the only one in the world, traveling through space and time. That's why it's critical to keep your connections to loved ones active.

Be on Facebook while you are traveling. You may not have internet a lot of the time, or the internet will be poor. Consider paying to have your phone be a hotspot. It's a little bit of money per month, but it's worth it and has saved me from being without internet. I love the convenience of it, and you will too.

Plan your journey around visiting family members or friends you haven't seen for a long time, or people that are good friends. When you see people you know, it will ground you, so you can continue traveling.

Check in by phone with loved ones. They worry about you, and it's good for both of you to stay connected no matter where you are.

Consider traveling with a pet. I started my trip with my beloved 14-year-old sheltie named Sadie. She didn't make it to the end of the trip. I lost her to bladder cancer about four months in. My Sadie was special, and I will never forget my first traveling buddy.

It took me a solid year to decide on getting another dog. I poured over profiles of rescue dogs, looking for a little buddy I could take care of. Best Friends Animal Society in Kanab, Utah, had my perfect match. I now have Rosie, an 8 year-old sheltie that looks just like Sadie and has many of the same mannerisms. Life is good again.

I highly recommend Best Friends Animal Society if you are looking for a pet. They have 3000 acres and house up to 1600 animals at one time including dogs, cats, horses, pigs, and just about everything else. The dedicated people at Best Friends are wonderful both to you, and your potential pet.

Travel tip: One of the easiest and best ways I stay connected while traveling is to offer to take a photo for someone I don't know. Many couples, families, or singles would love to have more pictures of themselves traveling. It's an easy and quick way to have a connection with a fellow traveler, and it's good manners too.

Practical matters:

You need to have an address to send your mail to. Keep in touch with whomever is nice enough to do this for you.

You will also need to come back occasionally to register your car, vote, go to doctor visits, and take care of any other business. You can't leave it all behind, as tempting as that may be.

Bad things that happened:

Remember when I said you need to take spontaneity with you on your trip? Well, there were many times when I used my spontaneity skillset.

The government shutdown happened smack dab in the middle of my travels. That meant that all of the National Monuments were closed. I did a lot of driving and circling around.

I also did a lot of circling around trying to avoid natural disasters. I traveled through Paradise, California shortly before a massive fire happened there. I tried to travel through the area again but was pushed out by massive flooding. My latest event was camping in Canyonville, Oregon and waking up to flames creeping down the hillside. That was day one of the Canyonville fire.

Besides being driven out by natural disasters, sometimes I was driven out by rude people. Many times it was centered around my furry traveling companion. I believe there are really only two types of people, those who love animals and those who don't.

When people see me walking my beautiful, sweet, elderly dog, they either come up and pet her, or they say something harsh.

One incident was a woman, a total stranger, who came up to me smiling down at Sadie and asked how old she was. I replied, "She is 13 and a half years old." The woman replied very curtly "She needs to be put down." Sadie was walking around, alert, and happy, and yet this woman wanted me to end her life because she was old.

Speaking of animals, several times I came very close to driving into an animal on the road. I can't stress enough how many times this will happen to you, and all I can say is, be alert at all times while you are driving. When you travel a lot of miles, you will get tired, so stop and smell the roses, and try not to drive at night.

Good things that happened:

One of the sheer joys of taking a road trip is the unpredictability of it. You never know what you will see. I am originally from Oregon, and bears are not a common sight. So, while driving high up in the Blue Mountains, I looked over and saw a bear! So exciting! He didn't stay for long, kind of shy, but so cute. I love animals, so to see the rich and wonderful amount of wildlife in our country gladdened my heart.

I met many great people on my trip, from all walks of life. They were a walking, talking advertisement for our beautiful country. I smiled at them, and they smiled back. We are all Americans, and we are all part of the human race. When you meet people across the country, you realize just how important it is to get to know your fellow citizens, and learn more about how they view the world and our country.

I have to give a special shout-out to the many dedicated people, often volunteers, who staff our state and national parks and monuments. They work tirelessly to ensure the health of our natural resources, and help travelers enjoy their visit. The same is true of the many people who staff the museums in small towns and large cities. They enjoy history, like I do, and it shows in their smiles.

Along with wonderful people, I have seen an America that is spectacularly beautiful, with open prairies, majestic mountains, and crystal clear rivers. I have seen a small fraction of the history of our country. I have seen the memorials to the brave people who shaped our country. I have fallen in love with America in a way that was not possible sitting in my living room. People ask me, "would I do it again?" The answer comes easily, "Yes, in a heartbeat."

Bibliography & Further Reading

Bodie State Historic Park, California State Parks, 1988.

Bottjer, Linda J. *Gold Rush Ghosts of Placerville, Coloma, and Georgetown*. Haunted America, a Division of The History Press, 2014.

Captain Jack's Stronghold Historic Trail, Lava Beds Natural History Association

Carey, John, *Eyewitness to History*, Harvard University Press, 2003.

Carmel Mission Basilica Map and Guide, Carmel Mission

Columbia State Historic Park, California State Parks

Donner Memorial State Park, California State Parks, 2014.

Dwyer, Jeff. *Ghost Hunter's Guide to California's Gold Rush Country*. Pelican Pub., 2009.

Enss, Chris. *Tales behind the Tombstones*. Morris Pub., 2007.

Ferndale City Guide, Ferndale Merchants Association, 2023.

Finch, etc. al.., Jackie. *Eyewitness Travel USA*. DK Publishing, 2017.

Fort Ross State Historic Park, California State Parks, 2001.

Geissinger, Terri Lynn. *Bodie*. Arcadia Publishing, 2009.

Glassman, Steve. *It Happened on the Santa Fe Trail*. Twodot, 2008.

Hill, William E. *The Oregon Trail, Yesterday and Today: a Brief History and Pictorial Journey along the Wagon Tracks of Pioneers*. Caxton Press, 2014.

Lava Beds , National Park Service

Lava Beds National Monument, National Park Service

Marcy, Randolph, *The Prairie Traveler, 1859*.

Margolin, Malcolm. *Life In A California Mission*. Heyday Books, 1989.

Marshall Gold Discovery, California State Parks

Mayo, Matthew P. *Haunted Old West: Phantom Cowboys, Spirit-Filled Saloons, Mystical Mine Camps, and Spectral Indians*. Globe Pequot Press, 2012.

McLaughlin, David, *Soldiers, Scoundrels, Poets & Priests*, Pentacle Press, 2018.

Old Mission San Juan Bautista Museo, Mission San Juan Bautista, 2012.

Rarick, Ethan. *Desperate Passage: the Donner Party's Perilous Journey West*. Oxford University Press, 2009.

Rutter, Michael. *Bedside Book of Bad Girls: Outlaw Women of the American West*. Farcountry Press, 2008.

Scott, Robert. *Plain Enemies: Best True Stories of the Frontier West*. Caxton Printers, 1995.

Senate, Richard. *Ghosts of the California Missions*. Shoreline Press, 2011.

Soledad Mission Brochure, Soledad Mission.

Sonoma State Historic Park, California State Parks, 2002.

Sutter's Fort, California State Parks

Teggart, Frederick. *Diary of Patrick Breen*. Vistabooks, 2017.

Wagner, Tricia Martineau. *It Happened on the Oregon Trail: Remarkable Events That Shaped History*. GPP, 2014.

Welcome to Mission San Francisco de Asis, Mission Dolores

Welcome to Old Mission San Jose, Mission San Jose.

Welcome to Old Mission San Juan Bautista, Mission San Juan Bautista.

Index

Referenced by Sections

About the Author

Julie Bettendorf is a world traveler with a degree in archaeology and a background in history. She has traveled extensively throughout Egypt, Central America, South America, Europe, and the United Kingdom, visiting archaeological and historical sites all along the way.

Currently, Julie is traveling around the US visiting ghost towns, ancient rock art sites, and archaeological wonders as part of research for her ongoing historical travel series entitled ***Wandering Woman***. Wandering Woman is a set of state-by-state guides, full of photographs, historical anecdotes, and unique tips to help other women travel and explore solo across the US by car. Julie enjoys writing freelance blogs, traveling frequently with her two adult children, and hiking outdoors with her faithful dog companion Rosie.

Also by Julie Bettendorf

Wandering Woman: Northern California is the twelfth book in the ***Wandering Woman Travel Series***. The first eleven books ***Wandering Woman: Montana***, ***Colorado, Utah, Nevada, Arizona, Oregon, Washington, Idaho, New Mexico, Wyoming, and Southern California*** are available in ebook and paperback.

Julie has published two children's books in an ongoing, beautifully illustrated travel series entitled ***Anthony Ant Goes to France*** and ***Anthony Ant Goes to Egypt***.

She has also published a work of historical fiction entitled ***Luxor: Book of Past Lives*** which has recently been released as an audiobook, read by renowned narrator Barry Shannon.